A Barnstormer Aviator

My personal journey

To scarf and goggles flying in the 1930s

Nick Vuyosevich

with

Nina Anderson

Copyright ©2018 by Safe Goods

All Rights Reserved

No part of this book may be reproduced in any form without the written consent of the publisher.

ISBN 978 1513637075

Library of Congress Catalog in Publication: 2018946664

Printed in the United States of America

Editor: Susan Butler

Published by Safe Goods

561 Shunpike Rd.

Sheffield, MA 01257

safe@bcn.net

www.SafeGoodsPublishing.com

Table of Contents

What readers say:

Only thirty years after Kitty Hawk a high school boy is dreaming of flight; first solo in the 1930s; and buying his first airplane for $189.00. This true story written by a New Jersey biplane pilot, is filled with names, places, aircraft and adventures from the golden era of aviation! What a fun read. - James P. Adams, ATP, Gold Seal Flight Instructor, Retired FAA Operations Inspector, FAASTeam Program Manager

My grandfather, Don Hall, was the designer of Lindbergh's airplane, the Spirit of St. Louis, so I have a vested interest in early aviation. This book gave me insight to the circuitous path most pilot wannabees, who were just part of the general population, had to follow to learn to fly. I loved the misadventures, calamities and comradery depicted among the early aviators that Nick described. While reading it I was transported back to the 1930s and got an in-person glimpse of the era my grandfather lived through. - Nova Hall, author of <u>Spirit and Creator, The Mysterious Man Behind Lindbergh's Flight to Paris.</u> [Safe Goods Publishing]

General aviation pilots from the 1920s and 30s are at times overlooked especially those from New Jersey. As the industry grew in New Jersey, few chronicled the struggle to provide flight schools, airports and flying clubs for would-be aviators seeking to fly those incredible scarf and goggles machines. This book describes the trials and tribulations, adventures and misadventures, and the insider stories of early aviators such as Clarence Chamberlin, Eddie Gorski, Chet Coons and George Stone. Documented with original photos, this book is an archival treasure of New Jersey flying in the golden age of aviation. - Ralph Villecca, Executive Director, Aviation Hall of Fame & Museum Of New Jersey

Foreword.

I became a pilot in 1967, eventually flying as a professional. People have asked me how I became interested in aviation. While my father gave up flying during World War II  he always took his first-born toddler to airports to watch the airplanes. My mother also soloed but gave it up after she went into a cloud and realized it wasn't the nice fluffy harmless creature she saw from the ground. But it wasn't until I met my first husband Neil that the subliminal love for aviation began to surface.

I was a senior in college and not sure of what I wanted to do after graduation. Back in the sixties women were not encouraged to do anything else but marry and clean house. Neil was a charter pilot and took me on a freight run to JFK (back then it was called Idlewild). My comment was, "you get paid to do this?" That started my quest with enthusiastic support from my Dad.

In 1980 when I was flying jets for Philip Morris I asked Nick to write down his memories of flying back in the twenties and thirties. This book is what he put together – single spaced on a typewriter with all the type corrections overlaid in ink (no white out back then)! Upon reading it, I realized what a miraculous thing it was for an immigrant's son with nary a nickel in his pocket to realize his dream of flying back in the days of early flight.

Dad collected a myriad of newspaper clippings from aviation events back then and I have included many of them in this book. He also took photos – few of the family – mostly of airplanes and pilots. His story is unique from an aviation history per-spective. We have heard about the war heroes, the record setters and the early aircraft designers. But rarely do you read about the young kids who looked skyward and struggled to reach their dream of being a pilot, especially when there were few flight schools and fewer instructors. What they went through, what they flew and how they achieved their dream is what this story tells.

Dad was instrumental in starting the Jersey City Flying Club with 60 members and not one pilot among them – just pilot wannabees! While flying out of Teterboro, he also was a key player in Clifton and Whippany Airports. Back then crashes and near crashes were common, and Dad tells several personal stories about his misadventures, which luckily, he survived. He was one of the charter members of the Aviation Hall of Fame of New Jersey, member of the Quiet Birdmen, Silver Wings and OX5 club. Please take a journey back with me into the early days of biplanes, barnstorming, air-shows and lots of smiles. This is written in my father, Nick Vuyosevich's words.

-Nina Anderson

A portion of the profits from this book will be donated to the New Jersey Aviation Hall of Fame.

www.njahof.org

Introduction.

In 1924 I was 15 years old and a high school student in Hoboken, New Jersey. Most every weekend I would start off on a long trek by hanging on the rear end of a trolley car that ran from Hoboken to Paterson via the Paterson Plank Road westward. As it slowed down at the railroad track at East Rutherford, I would jump off. Then I had a long walk along the railroad north about five or six miles to the Teterboro airport and the Gates Flying Circus with its renown pilots of the era in their colorful Standards OX5 with Hispano-Suiza engines.

The weekly show drew crowds from all over and with a couple of dollars crumpled up in my hands, I was constantly trying to sell the barker on letting me go up for a ride for two dollars instead of the five they were charging. It was a long afternoon, and nobody paid much attention to my two dollars. Toward the end of the day a pilot named Smitty waived me over. He took pity on me and allowed me to ride with him in a Hisso Standard for the measly two bucks. I was flying! I have never forgotten the thrill of looking down on my world from above and back at my hero behind the goggles who was responsible for transporting my body and soul in the sky. I had always dreamed that some day I would fly and here I was.

Some of the pilots of the day who all flew for Gates were Bill Diehl and Clarence Chamberlin (prior to his trip in the Columbia to Germany). Also flying for Gates were Tony Fokker (who was building a four-engine biplane at the field), Eddie Allen, Slim West and others of the "old timers" that I was later to have more than a nodding acquaintance with.

My first-hand experience at Teterboro fired me up to some day fly as a pilot myself, own an airplane and maybe an airport – all which eventually transpired. This was a glamorous period in aviation with flamboyant personalities abounding to carry aviation forward. Some didn't make it, but those who did made aviation history for our new breed of pilots to fly the incredible aircraft of today. For the next few years this was my spare time pattern – beg, walk, train, fly!

The Early Years

I was born in 1909 in New York City and lived in Hell's Kitchen on the westside of Manhattan. We lived in a five-story tenement with outside fire escapes for each family. And, there the kids would be able to sleep outside in the summer months and look up into the starry summer skies and dream. My fantasy was to get in the air and fly near the stars and moon. Being five years old I figured this was a definite possibility and made many trips above the earth in my imagination.

There were times when an occasional vintage plane roared up the Hudson River or overhead going someplace. When that happened, everyone stopped what they were doing and looked skyward. We were in total amazement at man's new dream come true in the early 1900s.

The first recollection of an intimate occurrence with flight was when my father opened the *New York Times* around 1915 and found a winning ticket to a free hydroplane ride around the Statue of Liberty and back to the starting point at 97th street in Manhattan. I remember his excitement and the good wishes from many of his friends in our neighborhood who saw him off that day in the Curtiss hydroplane. To me it looked like the Wright Brothers plane at Kitty Hawk with pontoons on it.

Of course, this made dad the hero around our block and he puffed a bit about his bravado and the fact that he had passed the "grand old lady" many times when he was quartermaster on a sailing ship. Now here he was so close in the air that he could almost kiss Lady Liberty's hand.

World War I came along and with it the thousands of stories of the romantic battles in the air. Stories of the airman of various Allies' Air Forces and of the enemy as well. War is like dog eat dog, but these recollections of mine at age eight seemed to be about the comradery of men, friends and foes that belied the purpose of war and rose above us ordinary mortals. Airmen seemed to be a breed apart and it was this exclusive society of men of the air that fired the imagination of the youth of my day by the thousands. Out of that surge of interest came a few geniuses who made the strides into this century with technological development, sacrifices and beliefs that made space travel a realistic accomplishment today.

During this war my mother died from the bad flu epidemic that struck the country. She was only twenty-eight and left my father with the problems of caregiving and feeding the seven children in a rough and tumble section of town. This was a tough time, and Dad decided to put four of us in the Episcopal Orphans Home located on 145th Street and Convent Avenue in New York City. There were many times while living there, that I thought of running away. The place was surrounded by high brick walls and topped with barbed wire. Because of this I fantasized about flying out of there.

I enlisted a couple of cronies to build me a glider in the unused swimming pool. I had seen pictures in magazines and books of gliders, and so then we fashioned one with the semblance of a wing and fuselage and tail. It was essential that I designed something I could wrap around myself and hold onto in the long arduous run off into space to get into the air and soar.

We had a shed with a ten-foot peaked roof at the home that divided the girl and boy areas. One evening when nobody was around, we managed to get the wood and window shade contraption up on the roof. I wrapped it around me and was ready for take-off. My vision was that once in the air I could get over that brick wall into the street on the other side and land. I could then run to the subway with the nickel I had hoarded for this purpose and get back to my Dad. Home sweet home!

The wind was blowing just right to take me there, or so I thought! All ready for take-off – I set my jaw and started down the slope in a quick run. Just about when I thought it was the appropriate time to jump into the air, I managed to miss the edge of the roof and took a nose dive into my friends. We all wound up in the clinic with bruises, but no broken bones, thank God. But, we were cured of flight for the time being until a more advanced air-craft could be built with better materials than the window shades we used.

The Dream Gets Closer.

My father remarried and we all moved to Willow Avenue in Hoboken, New Jersey. In those days a lot of German people lived there, and it was the cleanest town full of really happy people. I went to the same school as Frank Sinatra (who was a few grades below me).

As I described in the introduction I made my way to the Gates Flying Service where I got my first airplane ride for a measly two bucks. That was the first part of my dream to come true.

At that time, our family had a tough time making ends meet. Even though dad was a willing worker in construction, the pay was poor and the work hard and long. He was a master rigger and stone setter and was used to working in high places because of his time spent in his world travels on the sailing ships in the late 1800s. So, I went to work every day each summer as a hand in a mica plant on Murray Street in downtown New York City for S.O. Fillion Company. They made the central core for BG Spark Plug Company. I guess in a couple of summers I must have inspected a trillion mica washers for cracks and splits that would cause a plug to short.

When I was in high school in December 1924, the principal of the Hoboken High School announced that there was a job available for a young man with a New York construction Company as an office boy. Knowing of our acute home problem, I decided then and there to quit school and try for this job.

Dressed up spick and span and with a real stellar recommendation from the high school principal Mr. Allan, I was interviewed by Bill Deyerberg the controller of the company; and I got the job. My career with Walter Kidde and my intimate association with the top executives in the next twenty-five years started with the experience I gained as an office boy.

In this job I was in charge of filing papers in a small room at company headquarters. I must confess I wasn't quite up to figures and paperwork because my head was full of airplanes and ideas for building them. I constantly wondered how I could get into this activity. Several times I was caught drawing up plans for hangars and detailing out some form of aircraft that I thought I could build someday.

The executives thought this dilly-dallying on my part was pardonable and promptly decided that I could make better progress at their new manufacturing plant in Bloomfield where aircraft survival and aircraft fire equipment was being made for the Air Force and Navy. So, off I went to Bloomfield to work with machines for mundane aircraft components. Never did my thoughts drift from dreaming that now with some money in my hands I could learn to fly someday.

It Really Was Happening!

Aviation was stirring in men's souls. The United States began licensing pilots as a result of the Air Commerce Act of 1926. There was a feverish activity to fly the Atlantic and several expeditions were competing to be first. I recall of course, Lindberg's preparation and flight.

Then it was Clarence Chamberlin in his Bellanca 'Columbia'.

Then Admiral Byrd with 'Balchen' and Acosta in the American Fokker Tri motor.

Lindberg made it to Paris with his historical flight to be acclaimed all over the world in the Spirit of St. Louis – a Ryan with a Wright engine. And he came home to a hero's welcome.

Bill Hartig, VP of Crescent Aircraft, owned by Clarence, relayed this story to me about Chamberlin's attempt to be first against Lindbergh and the other entrants.

Chamberlin intended to make a solo flight in 1927 to reach Berlin, Germany with the maximum amount of gas he could carry in his Bellanca, "Columbia". At the Roosevelt field and just after Lindbergh had departed, Chamberlin's principal financial backer, Charles Levine, insisted on going along for the ride to share in the glory. At the last moment shortly before take-off, Chamberlin reluctantly agreed to take along this inexperienced aviation enthusiast. So, off they roared into the dawn on their way across the Atlantic.

ture, taken from THE NEWS plane, caught the Bellanca as she started out over the of waters for the long drill overseas. Clarence Chamberlin and Charlie Levine had never a doubt of the success of their plan on the start.

About mid-Atlantic, Clarence thought he could catch a few winks of sleep and handed the controls over to Levine who had a few hours of flight training. He told him to keep it on such and such a course for a few minutes while he rested. His blissful nap was aborted by the feeling that the plane was in a dive and being pulled up sharply. He found that Levine was trying to put the plane into a loop to achieve everlasting fame as the first man to do that over the middle of the Atlantic.

Chamberlin angrily regained control and berated Levine for acting so foolishly with a very heavily overloaded plane in the middle of the ocean. In no uncertain terms their friendship began a parting of the ways right then. Unfortunately, the added payload and foolishness of this incident contributed to Chamberlin's failure to reach his goal by a couple of hundred miles. He ran low on gas and had to put her down on a German farm.

Chamberlin's flight however, was a longer flight of around 4200 miles to Lindbergh's 3600. But this noteworthy flight was lost in the public acclaim showered on Lindbergh. Fortunately, Chamberlin was not totally forgotten. Upon returning to the USA, the mayors of over 100 cities in the U.S. and Canada invited him to stop at their airports for a welcoming ceremony. For this he selected a sporty biplane, a Sperry Messenger with a Cirrus engine. At each stop the city had its name painted on the fuselage and a gift was made to Clarence. I understand this netted him well over 100 grand! This plane was based in our hangar in Jersey City.

All these events kept us in high excitement as youths. Just before these notable flights I worked with others to form the Jersey City Flying Club.

JCFC started with 60 members, from ditch diggers to bankers, and not a pilot among them. I was chosen secretary of the club and remained so for nearly eight years through all the controversy, political musings and intrigues. The flying club got off to a good start and grew quickly to nearly 200 strong. We were considered a political force in the vote-conscious regime of the famous or infamous Mayor Frank Hague – of "I am the law" fame. He was really an aviation benefactor. He made it possible for Chamberlin to come to Jersey City with his

manufacturing plant, and he granted us the use of the 70 odd acres at the foot of Danforth Avenue on Newark Bay as a club airport. We thought it was only for seaplanes because there was a lake in the middle of the runway due to slow drainage every time it rained heavily. We had our work cut out for us to turn this mucky field into a usable airfield.

Since it was known that I worked for Walter Kidde construction, my job in those days was to plan for a hangar for five or six aircraft. I was caught drawing up plans for this hangar on company time! It was a fifty-foot span by seventy-five deep with a second story club room in the back for meetings.

But, it amused the Kidde executives and so they decided to help me with a framing design that used heavy yellow pine trusses for the fifty-foot span. The hangar was built and financed by members throughout several years during the depression.

In 1930 we had a deal with Clarence Chamberlain, "Mr. Teterboro", who was building and repairing aircraft at Teterboro. The deal was to allow him to store his aircraft at our field and receive in lieu of rent, flying time to be apportioned among the club members. This is how I got started with actual flying instruction – on Chamberlain's training planes with Army Air Force instructors that were on his payroll. The aircraft were Swallows with OX5 and Hisso engines 90-180 horsepower.

At the time instruction was started, there was a feeling that the loss of planes through the student's inexperience could be costly. The instructors were told just to give the novices dual time but never to solo them. Because no one would risk wrecking the aircraft, and because no money was being paid to the Chamberlin Company for aircraft usage, we had a bunch of pilots rolling up time far beyond normal prior to solo.

One fine summer day, Chamberlin's planes were actively selling rides at Jersey City. To promote the rides one of the pilots went up and barnstormed around the main part of Jersey City to announce that flying was going on that day and to entice folks to come and buy a ride.

Chamberlin had an instructor-mechanic who decided to go aloft and do the bit. He invited me to take the ride with him in a three-place Swallow biplane with a Hisso engine up front. This three-place job carried two people in the front seat. Being alone I had plenty of space to be thrown around during his attempts to scare the daylights out of me.

He loved to fall off on a wing from around 2500 feet and dive with wires screaming and wings walking back and forth straining. He took great delight in pulling out sharply, so my head disappeared below the cowling of the cockpit under the G-forces. After several of these dives I had given up hope of being a part of this future world!

He sure did attract a crowd that day. I could see lots of folks while looking straight down at the hangar wind sock which I swear he wanted to shear off just for fun. On his last try he just missed it. He zoomed over the Kellogg plant bordering the north side of the field jutting into Newark bay towards Federal

Shipyard to make a grandstand approach for a landing on the field.

However, we got into trouble after climaxing this wild ride by passing through the shipways heading for the field east with plenty of speed. In my humble judgement he was flying far too fast to get us on the ground in one piece. When he passed over the west bulkhead on the river end of the runway below the surface of the field, his wheels hit a concrete drain pipe shearing off the landing gear. About the same time I yelled, "get it up!" The engine roared as we added full power to get the nose up off the ground. But we smashed down again. This time it was without the gear and the propeller was shattered. I had my hand on the safety belt to get out in case of fire. The friction was throwing up smoke and dust; it looked like this was it.

The plane was skidding across the field and about this time I was thrown out sideways. I rolled and rolled a lot. Luckily, I wasn't hurt. The plane did not burn but lay crumbled up, damaged severely with the pilot slumped in the cockpit. I thought he was dead. When I went to see how he was I spotted an empty whiskey bottle on the floor. Now you can use your imagination to experience what my nose was going through with the foul smell of gasoline mixed with rye whiskey. He was dead alright – dead drunk!

Clarence and the gang poured onto the field to help. Neither of us was injured, but scratch one airplane owned by Chamberlin who was less than happy. Believe me, on all of my future flights with another pilot I always did a little more checking beyond the controls, wires, etc. I looked for a possible sustainer in the form of a whiskey bottle to give those daring carefree souls, called pilots, a bit of help to get to heaven quicker. Lucky for me Clarence had more airplanes.

I started to roll up dual time on these aircraft with an Army pilot named "Waspy" Sherman who was a little guy with plenty of guts. He was Chief Pilot for Clarence and we got along just fine. He imparted a lot of his skills during my lessons. Every time I asked if I could solo, he would say I wasn't ready yet. This was a stock answer to all the club members who were taking instruction then.

Chet Coons was Vice-President of the flying club and at the time was in the contracting business in Jersey City. He owned a Hisso Standard and an OX5 Swallow that he kept at the airport. He had soloed at Newark Airport in 1926 under instruction from a Captain Donaldson. Now the country was in a deep depression and nearly all the flying club members were out of jobs and begging for food in some cases. The club dwindled down to about fifteen men that had good jobs and income, with the rest in poverty. It was a pitiful period having to witness men, who had been your friends for years, willing to work but unable get jobs of any kind.

Chet did well and still had airplanes. And since I was still employed, we flew together all over New York, New Jersey, the New England states and Pennsylvania in a variety of aircraft: The Hisso Standard, Swallow two place with OX5 and Kinner engines, Waco, Great Lakes, Consolidated Trainer, Curtiss Fledging, Eaglerock, and other biplanes of the times.

Chet was a good pilot and he just couldn't take the fact that I was being stalled on soloing. He made a bet that I could solo his OX5 Swallow NC8732 in two landings. So, he invited me to go up with him. Upon making the second landing, he sent me up alone. It was April 3, 1933.

Chet sure took a chance according to Waspy, but I survived! I was on my way to getting my private license with Chet and his airplanes. We became fast friends for our whole lives.

Going for my Private Pilot test was a disappointment as it was postponed. It was 1935 and I had amassed around 55 hours. It was a beautiful clear day when I flew to Newark with Chet in the OX5 Swallow. We arrived with about six other students that were ahead of me. We just stood around and watched the proceedings. Each student came with their instructor and his own aircraft; no two were alike that day. The Government inspector, George Reams was an old Army Air Force instructor and a tough bird. He always walked around with an unlit stubby-end cigar in one side of his mouth and talked out of the other.

I think it was the second or third student he had that morning when he decided to ride along on this flight with the student. Most of us went up alone (as I did later that week). They took off in the two-seater on the long runway at Newark. When they reached about three-hundred feet dead ahead the motor quit. All of us were instructed that if that happened on take off to drop the nose and keep going straight ahead or risk spinning in.

Everyone of course, had eyes on this plane and were taken aback to see it make a 180 right back to the same runway. It approached downwind, hit the ground in a landing attempt, and bounced and bounced again. And miraculously landed right side up and came to a stop. We all rushed over as Reams came out of the front cockpit sputtering like mad and shouting, "No more flying today. I swallowed my God damn cigar".

Because my test was postponed, Chet suggested on the way back to Teterboro that I try a few spins in NC8732 which I had never done before. We climbed to 5000 feet over the meadows going north and I stalled it into a vicious spin. I did my normal movement of controls to bring it out, but it didn't respond. I tried again and no reaction to stop the spin. We were now down to 3000 feet with Chet shouting his head off for me to let go. Puzzled by my failure to bring it out I released the controls and Chet finally took over. He knew this airplane. We flew back up again and leveled off. He told me that the reason I didn't stop the spin was that this airplane was sluggish, not responsive like the Kinner that I had spun in training. I needed to keep the controls reversed much longer before bringing the stick back. I followed his instructions and finally got it right.

I later had time to reflect on what would have happened had Reams not swallowed his cigar that day and let me go up alone. The next time I came to Newark I made sure that I had my sweetheart airplane for the test – the Kinner Swallow. This was the most trustworthy and responsive to controls of any aircraft I had flown, and I knew it well. My turn came, and Reams told me to go up to 4500 feet and do a series of shallow turns and then 720 degree turns in both directions. Then at 4500 feet I was to enter a left-hand spin for two turns and come out in the same direction within a half turn of entry. Then do it right handed. The last advice he gave was to use the Empire State Building in New York City to orient myself for precision. It came off fine, and I finally got my ticket July 13, 1935. That was an accomplishment I had waited years to fulfill! My perseverance to beg, walk, train finally got me to actually fly and become a licensed pilot!

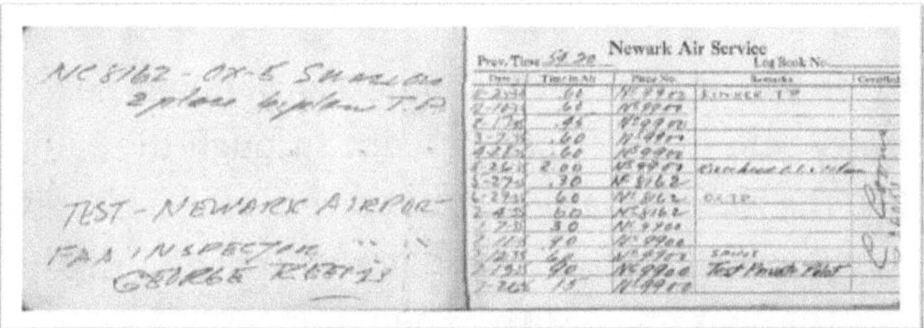

I only had a few hours on my private ticket when one Sunday while tinkering with the OX5 Swallow, a big man walked up behind me and introduced himself as Dr. Biddle of the Biddle Clinic in Jersey City. He asked me if I could just let him sit in the front seat and take him out on the runway for a faked take-off to impress some "show ladies" sitting in his nice white Cadillac car parked nearby. He just wanted to show them that he wasn't afraid to fly. Well, for ten bucks then I would shine his shoes. So, he got in and off we headed down field to the end of the runway for the mad rush and then abort without taking off.

This seemed to satisfy him. When I taxied back to the parking spot, he asked me to come over to the car to be introduced to the beautiful young women sitting there. He was quite the playboy and with six of Earl Carroll's Broadway Vanities he sure had the cream of "show ladies" hauling around with him.

After this first ride Dr. Biddle came down nearly every other week and we went through the same bit. The money was good, but after awhile it bored me. Finally, I couldn't stand it and took off into the air. This was my mistake. I had a screaming maniac on my hands. He was a big powerful man. Both of his arms were stretched out and his fists grasped the diagonal struts at the center section with such force that I was fearful that his strength would collapse the center section as we climbed to make a turn around the field.

Over the roar of the motor I tried to soothe him and to calm him down while at the same time making a shallow turn trying not to excite him more. I don't know who was more scared – him or me. Somehow, I made a long sweep and gentle approach to a landing and we just sat there. In time he calmed down and I was able to taxi in.

The girls just poured all around the plane and smothered him with their giggles and embraces while taking their conquering hero away. So, ended my ten-buck bonanza never to return.

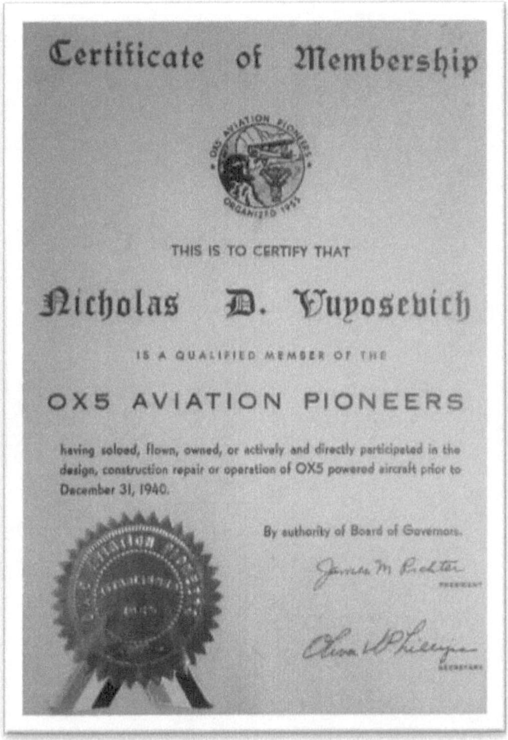

Trying To Stay Alive.

Every pilot must learn from their mistakes and are lucky if they survive. There was one such time for me. I was going out with a blonde model from New York and every good clear weekend in the summer we would take-off from Teterboro and fly to her sister's farm in south Jersey (below Woodbury in the tomato belt). Her sister's husband had a chicken farm, and alongside of his property was a long open field with an apple orchard on one side that I would drop into and take-off from. It was a short field. As long as a good wind was blowing down the runway I would have no problem lifting off in the Kinner with the two of us and make it back to Teterboro.

One exceptionally fine day having just completed a nice visit where we had stuffed ourselves with a great farm dinner. I decided to give the family members a ride. But when I got to the field where the plane rested on this calm evening, I had doubts that I could get off without a headwind. So, I asked them to meet me at the then-operating Camden Airport about ten miles to the north, so I could give them rides where I could safely depart with a passenger. Meanwhile, knowing this was going to be a tough take-off over the tall telephone wires strung across the end of the field, I took out all cushions, and luggage and loaded this extra weight into their car. We cleared out another couple of hundred feet of rough brambles and bushes at the departure end to give me more runway and had two of the boys hold the wings while I revved the engine up wide.

I was barely able to hop over those wires. Later they said they were sure I touched them as they swung about for quite awhile after I gained altitude. It was about five p.m. when I started the rides at Camden and as a result I got off with my girlfriend quite late for the trip back to Teterboro. It never occurred to me that I would not make it, but circumstances and bad judgement was to dictate.

The rules were quite plain back then that all aircraft without riding lights must be on the ground at six p.m. I blightly headed north following the highway system I knew quite well and was over Hightstown Airport around six. It was light up at my altitude of 2000 feet, but darkness was descending in the east. My girlfriend had a modeling job in the morning, so

I chose to press on against good judgement when I should have landed at Hightstown.

As I approached New Brunswick I could pick out the airway light beam at Hadley Airport still in operation at that time, and my horizon was fairly clear in the gathering darkness, but dead ahead rain clouds seem to cross my path. Before long a light drizzle surrounded us. Fortunately, we zoomed through and were back in the clear in short order. Once again, I chose to keep going instead of beating a hasty retreat back to Hightstown for the night.

My girl kept looking back at me and I could see through her goggles that her thoughts were to get down – anyplace but GET DOWN! But, No. I kept going north and as I followed the Penn railroad tracks at an altitude just under the scud I noticed the train cars were passing me. Boy was the head-wind strong. Now I became concerned that I wouldn't have enough gas to complete the trip as my bobbling gauge over the cowl told me we were getting low.

This made me decide to land alongside of the run-way lights at Newark Airport approaching from the south to the north/south runway. Since I had no radio I would be unannounced to the tower. Therefore, I couldn't tell them to turn on the runway lights. Since I violated the law and should have been on the ground a long time before, I was also worried that my license could be revoked. It was now night. I continued my straight in approach for the end of the runway in the darkness, flying by the seat of my pants.

I was 800 feet over Elizabeth, and then I planned to go over the meadowlands for my landing. My eyes were to the left looking toward the lightened sky over New Brunswick when my passenger let out an unearthly scream as she turned her head to see if I was still piloting the plane. It was then that I caught a brief glimpse of an airliner exhaust streaming along the aluminum fuselage on a collision course with my craft. That pilot didn't see us. I instinctively threw the controls into a right-hand dive, and somehow cleared the path for his safe landing.

I struggled to get out of my dive and back up for another approach. The lights came on for his landing and I figured the jig was up. I was scared to death at my stupidity and irresponsibility of being in the air and nearly killing ourselves and others.

I wobbled across the field flying over the tower knowing my gas was almost gone. I was hoping against hope that the controllers would hear me and turn the lights back on, so I could land safely. But the airliner on the ground was drowning out my feeble engine's roar as I made the left hand turn back to the south for another try. No lights! They didn't hear me; so now I was I was committed to get down. I had no more gas for a third try. Because the landing lights along the runway are a couple of feet high, I was able to use them as a guide to my landing and I got in. I didn't even know I was on the ground.

Quickly I taxied over to Eastern Aeronautical's hangar and was met by my good friend Gordon Hamilton. He was amazed that I came into the field so late. He then asked me to stay around until we learned if the airline pilots reported my presence in the air or if the Aeronautics folks called to learn of the aircraft that had just landed. No Call! Gordon was a peach for not reporting me. He said the ex-perience and my first night landing should be one I never forget. We young pilots sometimes feel we have nine lives while flying and I just lost one of mine. Gordon had my gas checked and told me that I only had a couple of quarts left in the tank!

I Bought My First Airplane For $189!

Back around 1934 Gordon Hamilton (owner and manager of Eastern Aeronautical Corporation at Newark Airport and later manager of La Guardia Airport), had just had the Sheriff put a sale ticket on a Robin. This was due to the non-payment of an engine overhaul bill being disputed by seven club owners. He turned to me that day and said, "Hey kid, if you want an airplane come back tomorrow and you can buy it for $189". I took him at his word.

I hadn't owned an airplane and now was a chance to get my hands on one that was a real beauty. I had been flying only biplanes up to this time and here was the possibility of owning my first monoplane – a three place!

The $189 might have just as well been $5000 back in those days because my earning power was not at that level. Chet agreed to gradual payments. Off to Newark we went on the day of the sale.

Arriving at Newark at Eastern's hangar we met a number of other people interested in the sale, including some airline pilots. But, what really surprised us was that our "friend" (and President of the Jersey City Flying Club), Charlie Sherman, professed no interest in the aircraft. He even promised us he would not bid on it. He was a big flamboyant man of about 35 years old at the time who was in the business of selling aircraft at Newark Airport. We knew his habits like a book including his con work that included issuing bounced checks that got him in difficulty more than once.

The Sheriff started off at $150, followed by $160, then $189. At this point Charlie raised it to $500. That got Chet mad and he said $750. Charlie and Chet escalated the bidding until it topped out at $4000 for an airplane estimated to be worth $5000. Then Charlie topped that bid with one at $4200, and the Sheriff sold it to him. My friend, Gordon Hamilton was standing near me; I quickly whispered in his ear that Sherman's checks were not good and he better demand cash. Gordon told the Sheriff who announced a cash only sale. Mr. Sherman said he didn't carry that much with him and offered to take Gordon with him to his bank to get the required money.

They drove off together and we waited. About an hour later the Sheriff came back mad as hell. "That four-flusher had me run around with him to four banks and none of them produced the cash," he said to Chet. "You can have it for $4000." Now I got into the act and said "Nothing doing. Let's start all over again". He reinstated the bidding and we got the airplane for $189. We trundled the ship out to the line, swung the prop and the old OX roared out, with Chet in the front seat and me in the back. Off we flew to Jersey City for what would be the beginning of a long wonderful couple of years with this aircraft as well as lots more stories to tell.

1935-38 Clifton, Whippany and Teterboro

Towards the end of the depression when Roosevelt turned the country around, we sold our interest in the flying club to the city of Jersey City for $20,000. There were only seven members left. When looking for the old contributing members who built the hangar, in order to give them their share of the money, we found many of them in want. We had a celebration and passed out the money to the group in a ratio to their contributions. Eventually a stadium was built on the airport grounds, known as Roosevelt Stadium.

With the demise of the Jersey City Flying club, Chet Coons and I seemed to drift apart seeing see each only occasionally. He kept flying biplanes and eventually owned a "modern" Stinson that he kept at a small field in Staten Island. I went on to other aviation interests and reconnected with people I had met in business at Kidde.

About this time, I met Lech Yejeski. He was a Polish Count and a civil engineer for bridge building. He had worked as a staff engineer for the famous American Polish bridge engineer Majeski who built the Poughkeepsie bridge, Detroit bridge and other well-known structures in the United States. He was promoting a new whip cream maker with a high-pressure nitrogen cylinder. He was at Kidde when I met him during negotiations for manufacturing this cylinder.

Although he didn't want to be a pilot, Lech was just as crazy about aviation as I was. He flew frequently with me in the Kinner. Later on, he put up the money for me to start a new aviation venture that included buying my Waco cabin with a 225 Continental up front. We also bought a J2 Cub for our primary instruction. The we formed a corporation called "Clifton Airport, Inc.", and leased 80 acres of farm land that was located directly across the river from Rutherford on the high bank overlooking the town.

Bootleggers had a mansion next to the field. But because I got along well with them, they allowed me to use their building as a club house for free. It was real ritzy – a good gathering place with a bar and light lunch.

I was then promoted to General Purchasing Agent at Kidde and my salary went up by $4000. This meant I could buy a good airplane. So now I was on top of my world. I was a bachelor with a really good income and airplanes!

The 80 acres we selected for the airfield was near centers of population growth. In time this was to become a bone of contention. For now it was just a big rolling, hilly farm field on top of a hill over-looking the industrial set-up at Delawanna and Rutherford. In my spare time I set about planning two runways, and a hangar for maintenance. At that time the planes were based at Teterboro which was managed by Eddie Gorski (later inducted into the New Jersey Aviation Hall of Fame).

In due time I had graded a sod runway north and south with good approaches to the field being 2600 feet long with a cross runway east and west of about 2200 feet. On the road side leading up to the field I had constructed a small one plane steel hangar to house the maintenance department with a small office and phone.

What I really had in mind was a country club for private owners and pilots at Clifton with a second outlet to gather the pilots from Roosevelt field, Teterboro, Holmes, Flushing and others to partici-pate in airshows here. It was an ideal spot with a straight stretch of Route 10 highway to park a lot of cars and room to set up stands for barkers. My vision must have been a throw back to my kid days when I was watching the shows of the Gates Flying Circus at Teterboro.

Clifton Airport made a few hundred a week by giving instruction and having charter flights to Atlantic city and Beverly Massachusetts. But we did better by giving rides in the summer. We flew folks for $5 each using the Waco, Kinner and Cub. The field was grassy with adequate length, and the approaches were clear. This meant it was lots of fun to fly out from that field.

We were running at Clifton every weekend and most of the maintenance we had to perform to keep the planes flying was interspersed with my time at Teterboro. Once when George Ray was flying the Waco on the day before our airshow, he made a particularly hard landing which snapped one of the members of the landing gear V's off. Fortunately, it gave way in the roll out and no damage was done when it dropped down to the ground on one side. We had to jack up the plane and remove the left side less the wheel. It was then loaded into the front seat of the Cub and lashed down for a flight to Flushing Airport, where Speed Hazlet could weld it.

Now aircraft weight and balance are a well-known important consideration, but in those days, we took it for granted that half of the strut projecting out into the slip stream with its V covering of linen, formed a slight additional wing. Once I was committed to take-off with only a 40hp up front, it started to yaw to the right. As long as I had full power on we had some climb — not much, but enough to do about 100 feet/minute. Strange things began to happen when I got to 500 or 600 feet, throttled back and turned to the left to cross Manhattan to get to Flushing. I found that the only way I could keep it going was to leave the engine at full power. This I did until I got over the field and dropped her in with extra speed to maintain some sort of control.

I was able to get on the ground alright. But when Speed looked at that little airplane and saw what we had done, he scratched his head and said I was born lucky. He cautioned me not to think I could fly the part back! He repaired the piece and had one of his mechanic's drive it back to Teterboro in a truck. I flew home all alone, with the Cub purring happily doing what it was supposed to do without all that extra weight.

Another time while back at Teterboro, Chet, Eddie Gorski and George Meyerhans were standing with me along the north/south runway on a fine summer day watching the planes take-off and land. In swooped our old Kinner Swallow NC9900 piloted by Stanley Bruno (he had bought it from us) who was operating out of the airport at Warwick, New York. He pulled up and he asked if we would like to fly it for old times sake. Such a silly question. I jumped at the chance and managed to put George in the front seat for his first ride ever in an airplane. Stan pulled the prop through and off we went into the sky towards the George Washington Bridge, which was under construction at that time.

What a beautiful feeling it was to take this old bird up after so many years. She climbed to about 4000 feet into the wind coming from the northeast. I did several simple tight 720 degree turns to give

George the treatment gradually; he seemed to be getting a big kick out of the pull up into a stall and off on a wing, and the pull out. This airplane had wonderful forgiving characteristics and was a great airplane to play around with. I never failed to get a thrill handling it. (I put in quite a few hours in it on barnstorming trips often with one of my more adventurous girlfriends.)

So, there we were at 4000 feet right over the cables on the George Washington Bridge, that had just been strung prior to decking, when it happened – bang! A loud and scary noise from up front. I didn't know what the hell happened, but the severe vibration promptly made me close the throttle and nose down and make a cautious turn back to the airport at Teterboro downwind.

George wasn't the only one who's hair stood up on his head, believe me! I knew I had plenty of altitude with a good glide range and thought I could make it by approaching from the south if traffic didn't get in my way. Whenever I tried to open the throttle, a terrific vibration occurred each time. Therefore, I closed it immediately. My thoughts were that a motor mount or two was broken. I hoped to just glide in to get on the ground in one piece. I was nervous but confident in my ability.

There were lots of student and low-time pilots practicing landings and take-offs that day. My main concern was to slide into the traffic pattern and to get down without running over some of the slower Aeronca C-3's ahead of me. In order not to overrun some landing planes in the middle of the runway who were unaware of my forced landing, I had to get into a nose high sideslip to hit the end of the south runway as soon as possible There were no radios back then to announce my plan.

Out of the corner of my eye I could see the gang still standing near the runway taking all of this in and wondering what the hell I was doing. Well, I lost altitude like a bloody fool. And because I thought I knew this airplane, I was a mite too late in bringing her out of the side slip to straighten her out for a landing. Inches were needed to not tear the tires off. But inches I didn't have. Both tires departed and ran down the runway ahead of me (as I heard later from the spectators). So, there I was running at much reduced landing roll on the rims about 500 feet from the approach end of the runway. This made it a very short landing roll - lucky for the Aeronca ahead!

Chet, Stanley and Gorski came running off to push the plane off the runway. It was then it was discovered that the top cylinder had blown the cylinder head and was hanging by the spark plug wire. Mr. Bruno was all shaken up about his airplane but very glad that I hadn't dropped it into the Hudson River. I was not about to do that since I couldn't swim, and I also hadn't known about George's faith in the almighty and his trust in my piloting ability.

Two years later one of Stanley's pilot friends at Warwick dropped the old Swallow into Warwick Lake at the end of the runway on take-off where she reposes to this day in twenty feet of water. The pilot got out OK which just proves my point; this was a most forgiving airplane. A real Sweetheart.

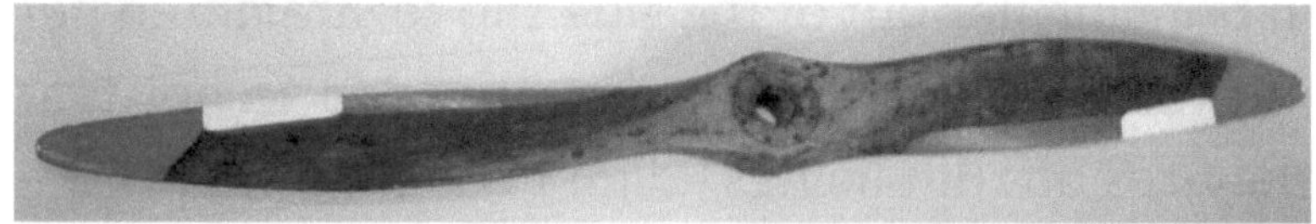

[*This is the prop from that plane. The propeller was replaced during an overhaul and Dad kept it and gave it to me.*]

Clifton Airport had hardly got off the ground when the public storm broke out to close us down. Industrials and citizens in Rutherford tried to stop me from operating. After a very rough year, and in spite of the strong support from the Aeronautics people and Gil Robb Wilson, the NJ State Aviation Director, eventually I moved the planes, the Waco and Cub, to Teterboro. Then I sold the Swallow. Once I stopped active operation of Clifton Airport and disbanded the staff I had, I sold the building, the Cub and the Waco. As the rent at Teterboro was eating me up I took to barnstorming on week-ends to pick up extra money. This venture led me to Whippany where after WWI a group of barn-stormers with old Jenny's and Standards operated on Haags Farm along Rt. 10.

Whippany field was used during the twenties by other rollicking pilots with their Jennys, Robins and Standards. Many were thrown out for drinking and killing a few passengers in wrecks there. It had been twenty years since the field was active. And the town was in no mood to let flying resume there for the week-end rides and airshows I had planned. However, I had foreseen this resistance.

With the support of the farmer, a Mr. Haag who had leased it previously as a landing strip, I finally got the town of Whippany to give us our license to operate. In return I promised the local American Legion to run an airshow to raise money for a new ambulance for the town.

I set up the airshow in August and in meetings with the Whippany, N.J. American Legion members, we detailed plans to use them to police the highway with the state police, park cars along the strip, build food stands and supply prizes for the event. The big prize was a charter flight to Atlantic City for three people.

The week-end selected for the airshow turned out to be ideal weather wise, and a real country atmosphere prevailed. Everyone was in a good mood to spend money and have fun. I had Speed Hazlet with his two-place Stearman and Charlie Stoffer (who was a famous Hollywood aerial stuntman) flying Speed's Stearman with a Wright J5 engine in it. Georgie Ray flew my Waco Y four-place with its 225 Continental. I flew the Cub mainly on low slow flights up and down the highway to attract attention. And besides offering rides I would be upstairs spinning and cavorting around with this little gem of an airplane, having a ball in the blue sky!

By the second day late in the afternoon, we had made considerable money and things were looking good. I was up in the Cub about 2500 feet directly over the field, where I was doing my bit with that 40 hp purring beautifully in a wing over and nosing toward the ground. I looked below and saw two red aircraft hit together on the ground near the take-off area. Thinking it might be my Waco I lost no time spinning to get down. Upon landing saw what happened. It was the two Stearmans, not my Waco thank goodness.

Speed had been waiting with his passengers at the end of the runway, when up from the blind side came Charlie Stoffer in the second Stearman (with two passengers) ready to line up for his departure. He didn't see Speed's ship and crashed right into him on the ground with his prop hitting the upper longeron steel tubing of Speed's airplane in the passenger area crushing and bending the section. But It was a miracle no one was hurt. Since both airplanes were damaged, the show was stopped. It also caused Speed to lose money from the event.

That's the way it goes sometimes; it is unpredictable. Otherwise the show was a real success and Whippany got its ambulance.

About the same time I was running the airshow at Whippany, I met Bill Lockhart who was a WWI ace from Canada and a sales agent for a large Pittsburgh electric company. He called me at Kidde and we ended up flying around together. When we were in the Swallow I'll never forget how I let this "Camel" pilot take the stick. Loch flew a Sopwith F1 with a Le Rhone engine in the war and took off from a gunship in 1918. He said that the Sopwith killed so many pilots because it was so tricky. And if you diverted your attention – curtains! He was amazed at how forgiving the Swallow was and he couldn't believe the advancement in aircraft technology in twenty years. He also flew the Cub and thought it was a marvel.

I continued to fly for the rest of the summer, but war clouds began to appear in 1939 so I knew commercial domestic flying was doomed to be stopped. Soon I began plans to liquidate both airstrips and planes.

With WWII approaching and civil flying being curtailed I finally sold the planes and flew in George Stone's aircraft. They were a Waco with a 300 Jacobs, a Twin Beech with full navigation equipment as well as a 400 hp Stagger Wing Beech.

I started flying with George as co-pilot on his business trips. He had the airplanes and was extremely well off. His father Julius Stone was a very wealthy industrialist in Columbus Ohio owning Seagrave Fire Truck Company, Columbia Chain, Black Diamond Coal Mines and other ventures. He was in his 80s when I met him, and we became good friends. George actually was the best man at my wedding to Gracie.

Westward Ho!

Most of the trips with George Stone were for his business on the east coast. But in August 1939 I was excited because we were flying all the way west to California. This trip was different. I had never been to the Canyon country and George had asked me to go in his Waco with a 300 hp Jacobs up front (NC14683). I had flown this airplane with him on trips around the east coast during May and June. Stops included Baltimore, Boston, and others. I had a similar plane with a 210 Continental in it that was based at Teterboro under my Clifton Airport company masthead. But, George's Waco had a lot more equipment for communication and navigation and had lots more zip and go than mine.

Following World War I new technology was developed to increase the range and performance of the radios being used to communicate with planes in the air. By now airborne radios were reliable enough and had enough power to make them viable to be standard in all planes. Navigation was mostly "I follow roads", lighted airways, and radio range beacons but we now also had ADF to home in on, a radio altimeter, a gyro compass. Some planes even had a Sperry autopilot. VOR's didn't come into existence until after WWII.

I flew TWA to Columbus to meet George and his two young sons for this trip. His boys were 12 and 14 and full of pep holding down the back seat of the Waco as we flew on to St. Louis by way of Indianapolis. We reached our first leg destination in about three and a half hours. The next day we headed for Kansas City where as we landed, we were met by Jack Fyre who was president and Chairman of the Board of TWA. George's business was short as he was anxious to get on the road to Amarillo via Wichita.

Soon we were flying over the oil derrick country of Texas which stretched for miles. This I had heard of but never seen, especially from the air. I marveled at the vastness of the oil industry spreading all over the Texas panhandle. We stayed overnight here intending to get an early start in the cool of dawn to try to get to Burbank by nightfall.

Dawn broke clear and cool and delightful. We had a fast breakfast at the Amarillo Airport and flew off westward to California via Albuquerque, and to Winslow and then on for a gas stop at Kingman,

Arizona. Up to Amarillo the flight was uneventful but fascinating as I saw the ever-changing terrain, lush farms, deserts and miles of oil fields. Uneventful that is, until we approached Albuquerque.

The country east of the Manzano mountains running north and south along a line east of Albuquerque had to be flown over through a pass leading to the airport. We were about fifty miles away when we faced a long line of thunderstorms that seemed to stretch about a hundred miles right on the nose. We were debating what was the best thing to do. We could see squalls in the pass and a few breaks between the thunderstorm formations toward the south that might allow us to get over the mountains and hit the airport in clear weather. Of course, since there was no onboard radar at that time, it was our eyeballs that gave us feedback for our on-the-spot decision.

We decided to go south to sneak through a break about twenty-five miles south of the pass. This involved moving over some very rugged terrain with few landing places if we had trouble. But, we pressed on and all was well. George's judgement was good for we broke out in blue sky weather swimming all over the Albuquerque countryside. A radio call to the controller gave us the green light to come in from the east and land. We were about five-hundred feet in the air on final when out of the blue came another Waco one hundred feet below us. He cut us off to land on the same runway. He never used the radio and landed just in front of us causing George to pull up and go around. He rarely lost his temper but this sure got George steamed.

We leveled off again, and called the tower asking who the crazy guy was that sneaked under our landing gear unannounced. It turned out that pilot had come through the line of storms from the north and just happened to converge on us at the same time. He was so emotionally shaken he forgot to announce his landing pattern. We landed and went to see the other pilot as he stood near his plane. Turns out he was flying a Goodyear executive from Denver. George had his say to the pilot who turned out to be a fellow Quiet Birdman from the Akron hangar.

When we arrived in 1939 Albuquerque was a quiet town with the desert in full bloom. The Harvey House was the place to stay and eat. We had lunch there and took in a few sights with the boys. We couldn't tarry because we still had a way to go to get to Burbank that day. Both boys by this time were close to me and it was a joy to have them along. The older one, Skip was always ready for pranks, so I had to keep a close eye on him.

Off again we climbed to eight thousand feet and later as we approached Winslow I wanted to see the Meteor Crater. Before long George flew over it. We had a good look at this natural wonder, and then off into the desert we flew towards Kingman to stop for gas for our final leg.

Toward the north of our flight path lay the San Francisco Peaks rising to twelve-thousand feet. Beyond them was the Grand Canyon where we planned to spend a few days with the boys touring in a car. It was a beautiful clear day and we could see for many miles. We had to climb higher and higher as the land was rising steadily from five-thousand feet and more around Flagstaff. Most of the land over in the direction of the Mojave Desert was a little lower, but George decided to cruise at ten-thousand in order to clear the mountains passing into Barstow and then slide down to Burbank.

This was the highest altitude this yellow bird of ours rose to on our entire trip. Out beyond the city of Burbank we could see many units of the U.S. Navy on maneuvers in the Pacific. Remember, it was just prior to WWII getting in full swing. Before we landed, we took a long pattern to fly over the ships. It took us a little more than two hours to travel from Kingman Arizona to Burbank.

The Francis family (George's in-laws) met us on arrival. I was taken in by the balmy climate, the flowering plants everywhere, and the easy pace of the people there. George's mother in-law had a beautiful home in Santa Monica, and it was there that we stayed. I remember stretching out in a hammock in the backyard, surrounded by palm trees shading me from the hot sun. I dozed off before dinner and woke up when the sun started to go down, and the cool breeze gave me a chill. I was too tired to get up so dozed back off. I woke up with a blanket over me (placed by George's mother in-law). Now warm, I fell back asleep.

Since they knew this was my first time in California, they made sure I saw the main attractions. We left the Stone domicile after several pleasant days and headed by car for Las Vegas and beyond to the Grand Canyon. George had reservations at the north rim and also a cabin at Kanab. We covered a lot of ground, visiting Zion National Park, Bryce Canyon and several sections of the Grand Canyon.

Our stay at the facilities at Indian Forest in Kanab turned out to be a real adventure for me. Several hundred tourists were there. At night after dinner, everyone gathered in the main lodge with its roaring fireplace going to hear the plans of "Uncle Billy". He was a vigorous gentleman of about 70 years old with a striking resemblance to Wild Bill Cody. He regaled about the west and invited all of us to go with him on a horseback ride through the Indian Forest to the top of the mountain to see "sun-up".

The corral had about sixty horses available for hire and crowds of kids were signing up for the trip. George's two sons asked him to let them go. They were both accomplished riders, but George steadfastly refused. They pleaded to no avail. Finally, they turned to me, their bosom pal by this time, and asked me to intercede. I pressed George and told him the tour was well chaperoned by cowboys and I thought they would be safe. George agreed to let them go only If I went with them. This delighted the boys but not me. I had never been on a horse and the last thing I wanted to do was ride those wild-looking mustangs.

Because the boys wouldn't let me say no, I went to Uncle Billy and told him of the predicament. He agreed to give me a very gentle horse and told me not to worry. I slept well that night assured that he meant what he said. The next morning it was dark as we all assembled at the corral, with the children making a mad rush to get their favorite horse. I tried to find Uncle Billy to see where my gentle horse was, but in the confusion couldn't find him. When the dust cleared and most of the riders were on their horses lining up for the start, a cowboy came over with the last nag – black, tall and bold looking. I told this gent that I didn't want to get on this wild looking thing as I would probably be tossed off the mountainside. Here again I was lulled by sweet talk telling me that there was nothing to it and that this was the gentlest horse in the group. So, up I went into the saddle and off with the crowd on the trail up the mountain trying very much to look like I knew how to ride.

Going up the hill was a cinch. All the horses followed each other, and rarely moved faster than a walk. And, if they happened to trot I held on for dear life in fear that I would soon be tossed to the ground. The cowboy behind me was the last man. I bet he had a laugh watching at my expense.

Soon we were on top of the mountain in a small meadow with everyone circled around Uncle Billy. The sun came up over the mountain spreading its rays over the forest below in the most spectacular sunrise ever. Finally, Billy bellowed "Boys and girls I'm going down the trail lickity-split. You see that log lying across the level stretch down there? Well, I want you all to follow me down. And when you come to that log jump it and gather to the left of it." So, with a flourish of his ten-gallon hat and his white hair flowing behind him, off goes Billy down the mountain trail with every dang kid doing the same thing.

It wasn't long before I realized I was alone on that mountain top with my courage now at the bottom of my boots. No sir! Not me! Off I slid from the back of that nag and took a long walk down with "Blackie" following behind. Boy did I get the razz berries when I finally arrived at that log gathering. But I was in one piece and that was that. The Stone boys never let up kidding me about it for years thereafter.

After the long drive back from our adventure in the Canyon, I realized that we had our share of fun and now all good things must come to an end as we had to get back. We left Burbank for home on the third of September. It had been a wonderful trip with good fellowship, friends and an awesome country to see. Off we flew into the eastern skies for home following pretty much the same route as on the way west. Nothing exciting but the country continued to fascinate us all. And, one never ceases to enjoy the scene of sky and earth from above in this little bird that faithfully carried us on our way.

We flew from Burbank to Winslow to Albuquerque to Amarillo with a stop at Tulsa, Oklahoma. We continued on to St. Louis where we stopped for some service work on the Waco at Robertson Aircraft's hangar. We got away early enough to plan a landing at Columbus just about dark. We hit turbulence after we passed Terre Haute, Indiana. Then an awful banging in the engine compartment started just as the sun went down. We were over farming country with plenty of spots to set down if an emergency ensued.

The engine had been running smoothly this whole trip, so the new noise had us concerned. The kids were sleeping in the back and George and I were trying to troubleshoot the cause. The turbulence increased as well as the hammering in the engine signaling that something must be loose up front. We throttled back and slowed down to ease the shock. I had rolled down the window on my side to see if I could notice anything outside of the cowlings. Nothing.

Luckily the turbulence abated just as soon as we were planning to land on a large farm below that in the waning light appeared big enough. George was about ready to release his two flares to light up the area for his approach when the hammering stopped, and he decided to try for Columbus. The boys slept through this whole ordeal. Landing at Columbus in the dark around nine p.m., we taxied towards the TWA hangar where a mechanic friend of George's was on duty. We relayed the noise to him. The mechanic opened up the engine cowl and pulled out a wrench. With a smile he chuckled and said to George, "How did this get in there?" The aircraft mechanic at St. Louis must have forgotten to remove the wrench when he closed up the cowl. That ended my first and most unforgettable flight beyond the Mississippi, which was to me the wild, wild west.

On a later trip with George flying to California, we left Columbus in a Stagger Wing Beech. It was a very fast plane of its day, and superbly equipped navigation and radio-wise. George was a very capable pilot in the Air Force and later in commercial aviation. I learned a great deal from him. Our first stop was Cincinnati. There we had met the publisher of the *Cincinnati Gazette* and his wife who were on their way to St. Louis in another Stagger Wing. Because the weather was marginal and because of the lack of instrumentation in his aircraft, he was hesitant to launch.

He asked George if we could fly tandem with him off our wing part of the way as we were going in the direction of his next stop for a meeting. Of course, George agreed and after take-off I kept him in sight from my right seat. The visibility was pretty hazy for the first fifty miles. Because he didn't have as powerful a ship as George's, we had to throttle back to keep him in sight. Finally, we got in the clear; he waved off and went on his way.

The trip was quite uneventful until we landed at a small field in Winslow Arizona. I think it was an emergency field having only a lone radio transmitter for navigation on the airway. As we landed and pulled up for gas we noticed a young boy of eight standing next to the fuel pump. While George was putting the fuel in for the final leg to Los Angeles, the boy asked if I wanted to see a rattlesnake. Now the last thing in the world I wanted next to me was this demon and I said so. The little rascal with a special stick in hand rushed off into the brush. I turned my attention to other things.

It wasn't more than a few minutes later when this little devil came back with the biggest, baddest snake I'd ever seen. It was dangling from a loop in the wire attached to his stick and he proudly announced, "See?". I damn near had a heart attack and said to his father standing there, "Do you think he is going to live to 16 if he keeps this up?" To which the man replied, "Shucks, he does it all the time and its good eatin'."

Well, with the excitement of the snake diverting our focus no one was paying attention to the gas going in the tank. It was a hot afternoon and the field was over 4000 feet in elevation. Because we were really overloaded for that altitude and temperature, George was concerned about taking off with the extra fuel weight. The runway was kind of short, so we cleared another hundred feet of brambles away from the departure end.

Off we roared and it seemed only seconds that I was thinking better of this, but George kept going. Sweat was on both of our brows, and the runway was fast disappearing behind us. She finally lifted off and hopped over the brambles at the end and began to climb. Once in the air this airplane had great climb ability! I didn't say a thing. But George broke the silence with "Boy, that was close!". I couldn't' say a thing. I just nodded my head. I was paralyzed.

On the way into Los Angeles we headed over the mountains and noticed a large forest fire spread out over the eastern slope. We were glad to have enough fuel to be high enough to stay clear of the smoke. My hat was off to Walter Beech. He sure built a sensational aircraft with enough power to get off in tight spots.

Well, WWII had begun and civil flying was just about dead. I was frozen in my job at Kidde because we were a Navy supplier. Years later I was part of the team that designed hardware that went up with the monkey on the first space capsule. I also worked on the escape slides for the first Boeing 707 and designed and built parts for nuclear submarines. I continued to fly a little with other pilots. This included flying in Frank Allen's Twin Cessna where I took my new wife and one-year old daughter for a ride in 1945 [see Epilogue]. When my second daughter came into this world, flying took a back seat to making a living, being a father and taking on the role of an opera Diva's husband. My wife Grace embarked on a professional career as an opera singer in New York City and much of my free time was spent at her performances.

The only flying I did after that was as an airline passenger and in the 1970s with my oldest daughter who became a professional pilot and let me take the controls of her Stinson 108-3 every now and then.

I did get a chance to sit in the right seat of her jet in the 1980s. Nina had a deadhead leg in Philip Morris' Hawker 700 and I was invited along by the Chairman of the Board who I knew from various social circles. Boy was that cockpit different from the Waco and the Stagger Wing Beech!

The early years of aviation was an exciting time to be alive. After that first attempt at flight when I jumped off the roof at the orphanage, I am proud to say that I begged, walked, and took the train to realize my dream – to FLY!

Epilogue

Dad's letter about my first flight.

"You were one year old. The date was December 9, 1945. The place was Caldwell Airport and the plane a Twin Cessna NC58085 with Jacobs engines. The pilot was Frank Allen with Dad as the co-pilot. You and your mom (a former student pilot) were in the back.

I was practicing a couple of landings in the company plane and after one of the landings we flew over New York City. It was there at 3000 feet that your mother passed you over to me and you sat in my lap with your tiny hands on the wheel pushing it back and forth with the plane porpoising across the Manhattan skyline, much to the delight of Frank and your Dad. Now look at you, flying bigger aircraft and making it your life's work.

As I look back at your early youth, it seems the times I took you to Teterboro to look over the planes was a lot of fun for you. I could sense a developing interest in airplanes even at that early age of five, but never dreamed that you would go as far as you have in aviation. Yes, you girls that fly are a breed apart. God Bless you all."

-your dad

Nick went to the hangar in the sky in 1989. He is always with me when I fly. – Nina

Nick and Gracie had three daughters Nina, Kim and Jeanne. In 2002 Gracie went to the stage in the sky (she was an opera singer)

Appendix: Nick's Training Manual

There were few printed flying manuals back in the 1920s so Nick made one for himself. These are excerpted pages from the original training booklet.

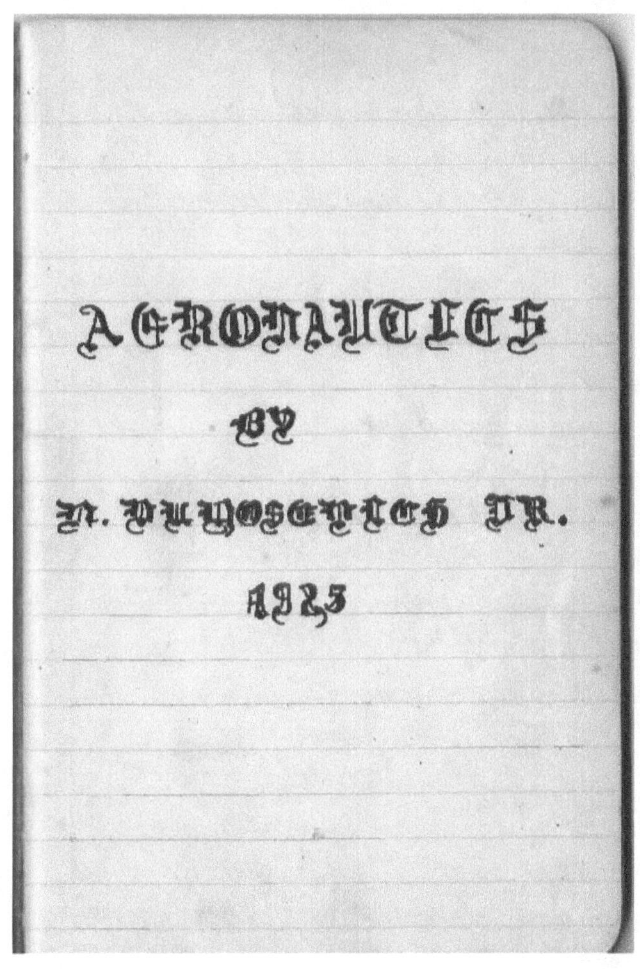

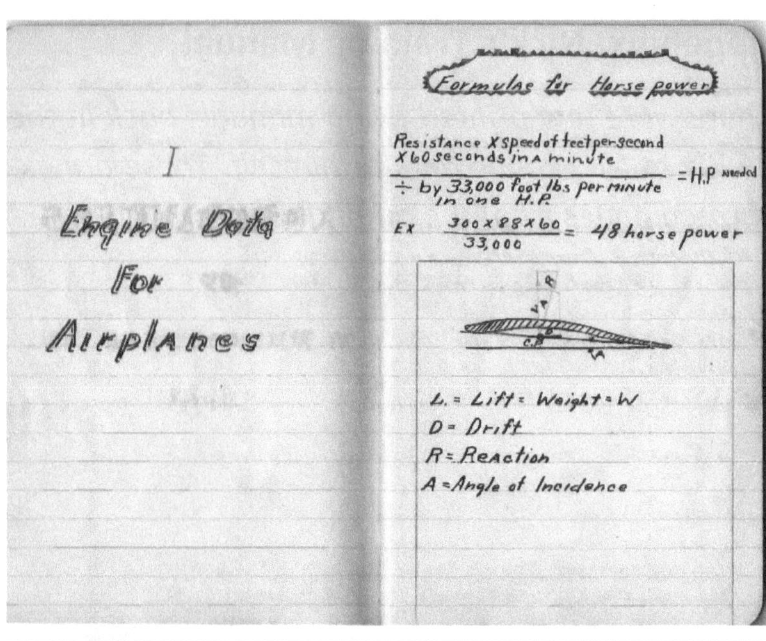

I

Engine Data
For
Airplanes

Formulas for Horse power

Resistance × speed of feet per second
× 60 seconds in a minute
÷ by 33,000 foot lbs per minute = H.P needed
in one H.P.

EX $\dfrac{300 \times 88 \times 60}{33,000}$ = 48 horse power

L. = Lift = Weight = W
D = Drift
R = Reaction
A = Angle of Incidence

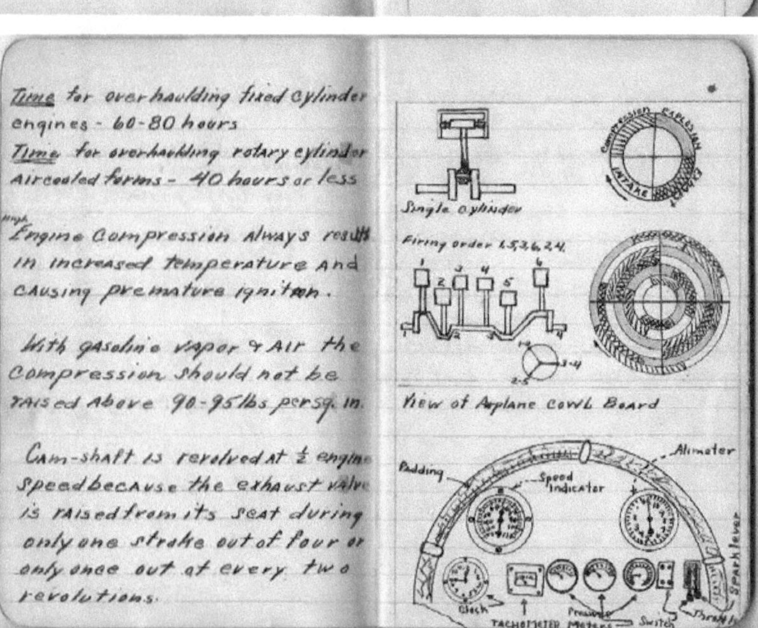

Time for over haulding fixed cylinder
engines - 60-80 hours
Time for overhaulding rotary cylinder
Aircooled forms - 40 hours or less

High
Engine Compression always results
in increased temperature and
causing premature ignition.

With gasoline vapor & air the
compression should not be
raised above 90-95 lbs per sq. in.

Cam-shaft is revolved at ½ engine
speed because the exhaust valve
is raised from its seat during
only one stroke out of four or
only once out of every two
revolutions.

Single cylinder
Firing order 1.5.3.6.2.4.
View of Airplane Cowl Board
Padding
Speed Indicator
Altimeter
Clock
TACHOMETER Meters
Pressure
Switch
Spark lever
Throttle

Usual compression ratio is $4\frac{1}{2}$-1
in other words, suppose the air space
above the piston to have $4\frac{1}{2}$ times
the volume when the piston is
at the bottom of its stroke that
it has when the piston is at the
top of the stroke.

A rich mixture can be found
by seeing black smoke issuing
from the muffler; the exhaust gas
having a pungent odor.

If the mixture contains a
suplus of air there will be popping
sounds in the carburetor; THIS
IS COMMONLY CALLED: Blowing back.

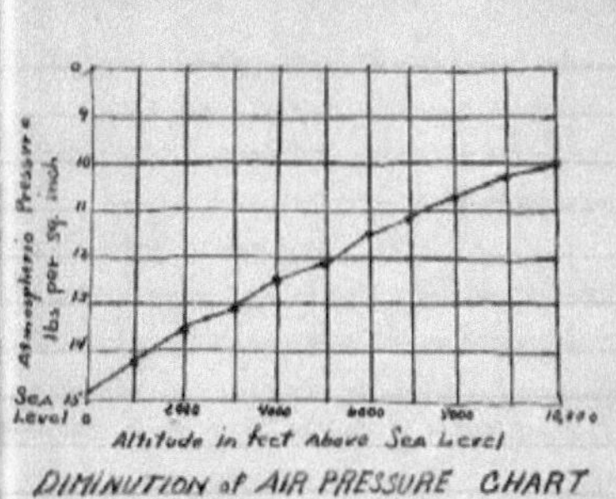

DIMINUTION of AIR PRESSURE CHART

MAGNETO

An armature winding of large wire
will produce a current of
great amperage but of small
voltage.
An armature with very fine wire
will deliver a current of HIGH
VOLTAGE but Low Amperage.

An excess of lubricating oil is
usually manifested by a bluish –
white smoke issuing from the
exhaust.

The cylinder bore should not ex-
ceed $4\frac{1}{2}$ or 5" and the compression
pressure should never exceed 75
lbs absolute.

Engines designed for high speed
should have the stroke not much longer
than the bore.
The disadvantage of short stroke
engines is that they will not pull
well at low speeds but run with
great regularity & smoothness at
high velocity.
the long stroke engine is
much superior for slow speed
work and it will pull steadily
with increasing power at low speeds
The longer the stroke the
slower the speed
Valve heads should be about
$\frac{1}{2}$ the bore
Tungsten steel is best material
for valves.
A settling basin for sediment should
be provided having a cubic content
not less than one tenth of the total oil
capacity. The depth of this basin
should be at least $2\frac{1}{2}$ inches and its
walls vertical to reduce the mixing
of sediment with oil in circulation

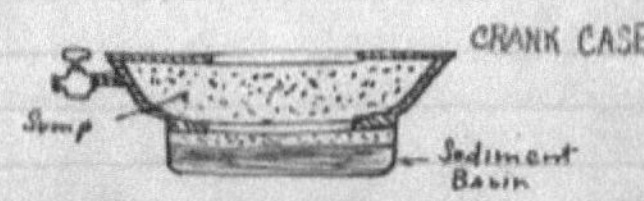

Best results are obtained by having the oil supply completely replenished every 5 hours of actual engine operation.

Crank shaft is usually made of high tensile steel of special composition made in 4 ways.
1. Drop or machine forgings
2. Blocking out of solid metal
3. Some are built in 2 pieces
4. Formed between dies

Airplane crank cases are usually made of aluminum it has about the same strength as iron with ⅓ of its weight.

Mobile oil no. B is recommended for Curtiss OX2 engine

Spark Plugs giving best results are extremely small with short points.

If motor is in use every day the magneto should be oiled every 4 days.

STANDARD S.A.E. ENGINE BED DIMENSIONS

Distance between timbers	12"	14"	16"
Width of bed timbers	1¼"	1⅜"	2"
Distance between center of bolts	13⅛"	15⅝"	18"

Reduction in maneuverability below a certain value would mean a lessening of safty in case of engine trouble and especially so on multi-engine machines.

Reducing of weight has led to different material to be used in bldg. of gasoline tanks: table below shows weight per gal. of gas of various metals.

MATERIAL	LBS. per GAL. APPROX.
Terne Plate	1.00
Aluminum (welded)	0.60
Duralumin, nickled plated, soldered & riveted	.35–.40

The use of metals at once brings up the problem of fatigue & corrosion. Protective coatings are recommended as follows.

STEEL TUBING – Interior protected by filling with hot linseed oil after welding.

STEEL ALUMINUM, DURALUMIN + two coats primer, iron oxide, or Aluminized varnish. Basic pigments such as red lead, are not to be used on duralumin.

ALUMINUM & ITS ALLOYS: when exposed in unusual service viz: in gasoline & water systems, and to salt water Z-D process consisting of baking in a water glass solution. This is used for carburetor bowls.

MAGNESIUM ALLOYS. necessary to prepare the surface, first by Parkerizing, forming a magnesium phosphate or dilute nitric acid; then apply enamel or duco.

ANODIC treatment for Al. & Dural. consists of passing an electric current through a solution of bichromate of

potassium, using the metal
as the anode. The current is
passed at 35 volts rising to 60
volts in 1 hour. Anhydrous oxide
is believed to result. This is
now undergoing extensive salt
spray test.

<u>PLATING</u> ÷ Cadmium plating on various
metals has proved as good with
a 0.0003 in thickness as zinc
plating with 0.0001 inch

THE RUDDER

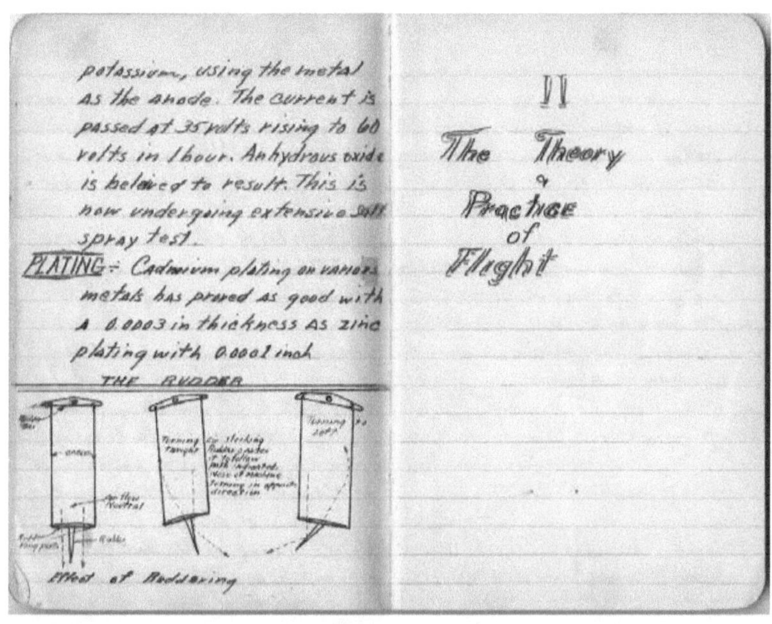

Effect of Ruddering

II

The Theory
&
Practice
of
Flight

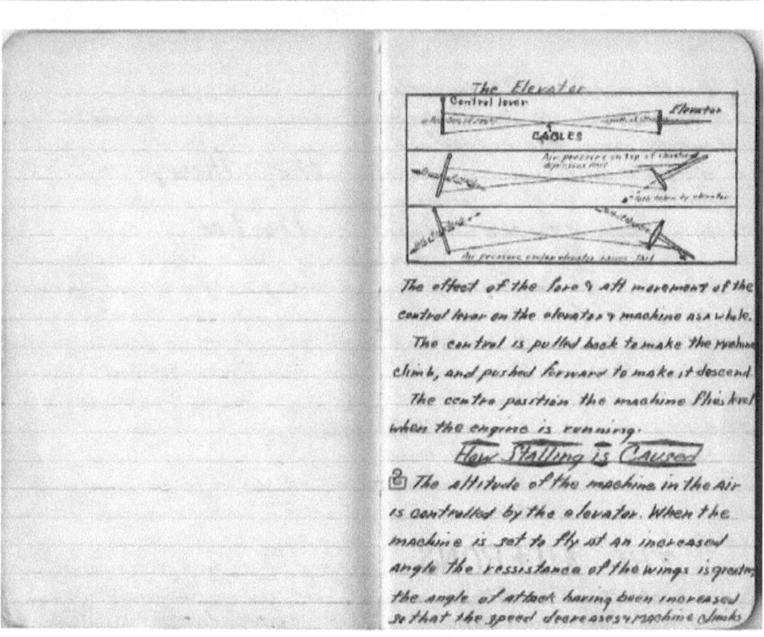

The effect of the fore & aft movement of the
control lever on the elevator & machine as a whole.

The control is pulled back to make the machine
climb, and pushed forward to make it descend.

The centre position the machine flies level
when the engine is running.

How Stalling is Caused

The altitude of the machine in the air
is controlled by the elevator. When the
machine is set to fly at an increased
angle the resistance of the wings is greater
the angle of attack having been increased
so that the speed decreases & machine sinks

⊡ When the machine is set by the elevator to fly downwards slightly, the resistance set up by the wings attacking the air is decreased and the machine increases its speed. Any increase in speed above the known amount the pilot will know the machine is falling. If the speed decreases he knows he is climbing. If he allows the air speed to fall below a certain point the machine will stall - He will lose controll and will only be restored when sufficient air speed is again provided. As soon as stalling is imminent about to occur he should put the nose of the plane downward to increase speed and so regain control.

THE AILERONS

Are controlling flaps fitted on each wing operates with the sideward

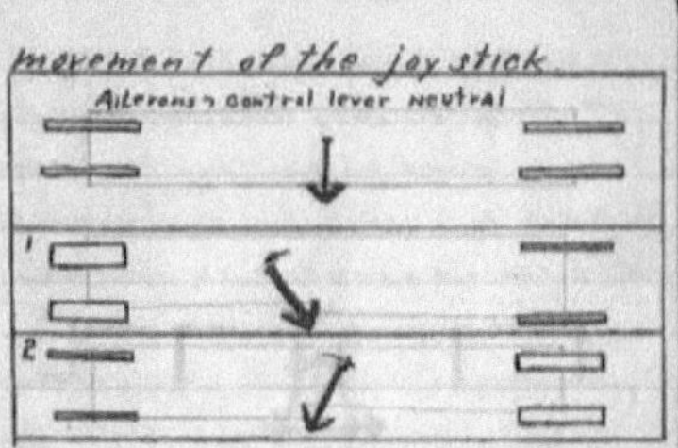

1. Control lever to left depresses right aileron and raises left causing machine to bank to the left
2. Control lever to right depresses left aileron and raises right causing machine to bank to the right.

⊡ The ailerons. The sideway movement of the control lever when it is pressed to the right makes the left aileron go down and the right aileron come up, whiche causes machine to fly right wing down. To make machine fly left wing down

the control lever is moved to the left. The sideways movement of the lever is used in banking the machine for turns and correcting the air bumps which cause a wing to rise or drop

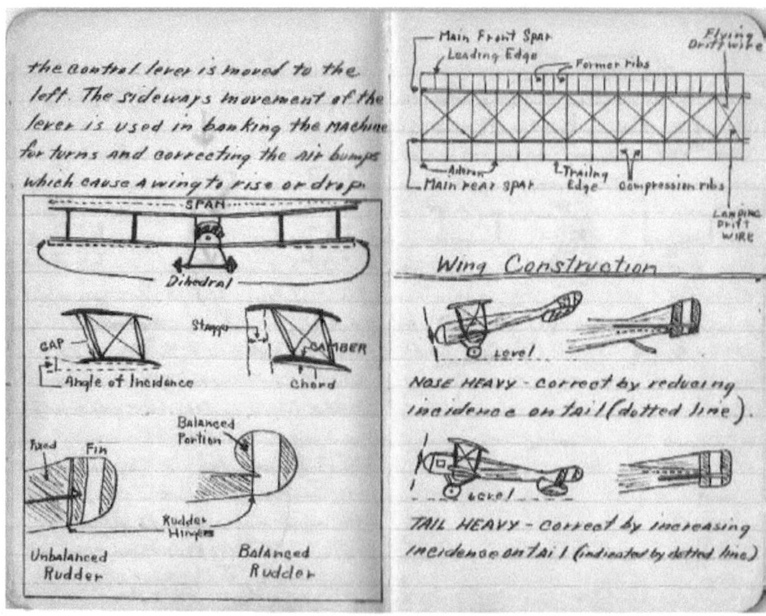

Propeller Torque

When an engine is blipped in the air it will be noticed that the lateral balance of the machine is temporally upset and one wing will rise or fall as the engine is switched on & off. This is due to what is called torque of the propeller. If the propeller revolves in a clockwise direction from the pilots seat. It creates an opposite turning movement of the machine which will tend to revolve about its longitudinal axis in an anti-clockwise direction. Unless due allowance is made for this the machine would fly left wing down. But to compensate for the torque of the propeller more lift is given the left wing by increasing the incidence or giving it what is called a wash-in.

This greater lift allows the machine to fly laterally level despite the torque action.

When the engine is switched off for descending the torque decreases, and so the left wing with the greater lift will tend to rise momentarily. When the engine is being "blipped" on the ground, the same sideways rock of the machine will be noticed. When the engine is on, the wing will drop, to rise again level as soon as switch is off.

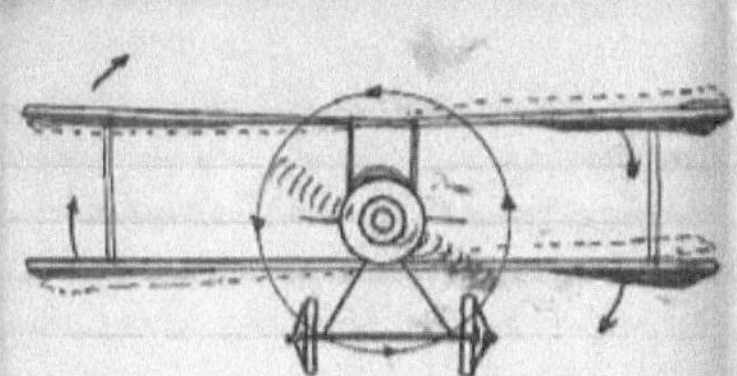

Dotted line shows how the left wing with the increased incidence rises when engine is switched off.

The torque of a clockwise-running engine or propeller tends to make machine turn in an anti-clockwise direction i.e. to fly left wing down. This tendency is counteracted by a wash or increase in incidence on the left wing as shown by the thickened portion in the sketch. The dotted line shows what happens when the engine is switched off in the air, and causes the left wing to rise momentarily owing to the disappearance of the propeller torque.

Dirigible Data

Shenandoah was 680' long 76.78' in diameter with a gas capacity of 21,148,000 cubic feet. Approximate weight as follows.

Frame	58,250 lbs
Envelopes	11,000 "
Motors & Cars	7,800 "

Ship had 20 gas cells the outer & inner coverings of gold-beaters skin, a substance from the outer skin of the blindgut of the ox. Material taken from 900,000 oxen.

Lifting power of hydrogen gas is as follows.
1 cu. ft of air weighs   1.293 K. g.
" " " of hydrogen "   .089 K. g.
" " " hydrogen lifts   1.204 K. g.
   35.31 cu. ft lifts 1.2 x 2.2046 = 2.65 lbs
1,000 cu. ft lifts $\dfrac{1,000 \text{ or } 2.65}{35.31}$ = 75.00 lbs.

Helium lifts 92% of hydrogen.
Lift of helium gas 92% of 75 = 69 lbs
per 1,000 cu. ft.
  Total lift of the Shenandoah
with helium 150,212 lbs.

DIAGRAMS
OF CONTROLS ON A
WELL KNOWN PLANE.

Rudder

Elevator

Stick

Elevator

Aileron

Pulleys

Rudder Bar

L. S. P.

DIMENSIONS OF A LINCOLN SPORT PLANE

Span	20'
Chord both wings	34"
Gap between wings	40"
Stagger	15"
Length over all	16'
Height over all	5' 7"

WINGS

Wing curve U.S.A	27
Total wing area	108 sq. ft.
Angle of incidence, bottom wing	0 deg
" " " , top wing	1½ deg.
Decalage,	1½ deg
Dihedral both wings	4 deg

Tail Unit

Stabilizer area	7½ sq. ft.
Elevator "	5½ " "
Fin "	3 " "
Rudder "	3 " "
Aileron " (each)	6 " "

Weight

Weight empty	370 lbs.
" loaded full	600 "
Wing loading per sq. ft.	5½ lbs
Power loading per H.P.	17 "

Power Plant

Anzani 3 cycle 30-35 H.P. (preffered)	
Propeller, 6' dia. 5½' pitch	
" speed 1,500 r.p.m.	
Oit capacity 5 qts	
Gas " 6 gals.	

Performance with full load.

Max. speed	90 m.p.h.
Cruising "	75 " " "
Minimum "	35 " " "
Range	250 miles
Miles per gal. gas	35 "
Climb ft per minute	800'
Factor of safty	11

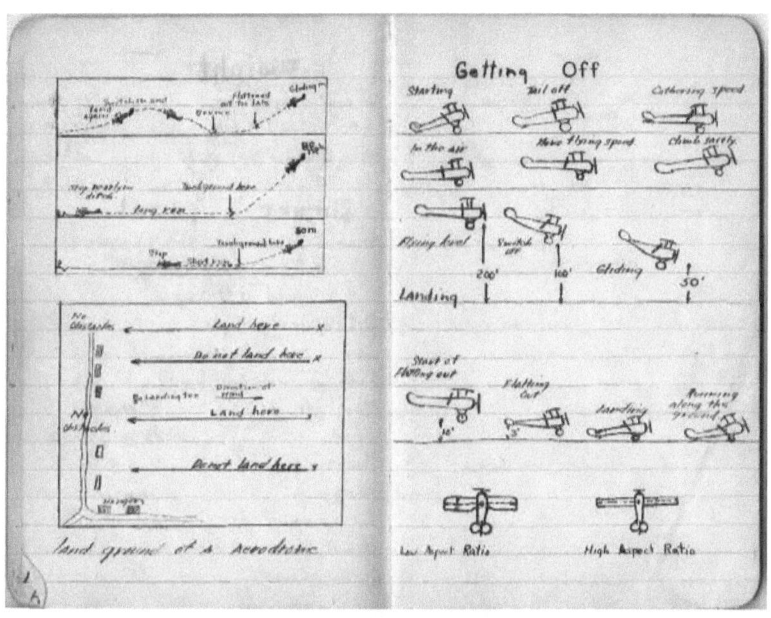

For a PDF copy of the entire manual in a larger form that is easier to read, please go to:

http://foreveryoungcooperative.com/19aeinmalisp.html

or call us at 888-217-7233

About the authors:

Nick Vuyosevich *was born to a Yugoslavian immigrant and was one of seven children. His story has been told in this book. After WWII his aviation endeavors mostly pertained to manufacturing survival equipment for aviation and submarines. In 1950 he started his own business, V Associates, continuing to produce parts for the military and sub-contractors. He was married to Grace Leng who enjoyed a professional career as an opera singer with the New York City Opera Company. They had three daughters (Nina, Kim and Jeanne) and two grandchildren and since 1956 lived in Monmouth County, New Jersey.*

Nina Anderson *was the first-born daughter of Nick and Grace. She followed in her father's footsteps becoming the first New Jersey female corporate pilot flying jets. Nina soloed in 1968 and worked as regional airline pilot before being hired by Philip Morris to fly out of Teterboro, NJ in 1980. Nina retired from professional flying in 2008 but still flies light aircraft out of Great Barrington, MA. She is author of 18 books on natural health and aviation and currently produces an electrolyte drink for pilots and sports enthusiasts. (www.electroblast.com). She collaborated with Nick on this book and put it together with the photos he supplied.*

Other Books by Safe Goods

Aviation:

2012 Airborne Prophesy	$ 16.95
Flying Above the Glass Ceiling	$ 14.95
Spirit & Creator (Spirit of St. Louis)	$ 29.95
The Backseat Flyer	$ 8.95

Health books:

Nutritional Leverage for Great Golf	$ 9.95
Overcoming Senior Moments Expanded	$ 9.95
Prevent Cancer, Strokes, Heart Attacks	$ 11.95
Cancer Disarmed Expanded	$ 7.95
Eye Care Naturally	$ 8.95
Aaargh! Menopause	$ 9.95
Live Longer with Cellular Rejuvenation	$ 9.95
Think and Feel Younger	$ 9.95

www.SafeGoodsPublishing.com